BLAZERS

MONSTERS

Mummies

by Jennifer M. Besel

Reading Consultant:
Barbara J. Fox
Reading Specialist
North Carolina State University

Content Consultant:
David D. Gilmore
Professor of Anthropology
Stony Brook University
State University of New York

Capstone
press

Mankato, Minnesota

Blazers is published by Capstone Press,
151 Good Counsel Drive, P.O. Box 669, Mankato, Minnesota 56002.
www.capstonepress.com

Library of Congress Cataloging-in-Publication Data
Besel, Jennifer M.
    Mummies / by Jennifer M. Besel.
    p. cm.—(Blazers. Monsters)
    Summary: "Describes the history and myths of mummies, their features,
and their place in popular culture"—Provided by publisher.
    Includes bibliographical references and index.
    ISBN-13: 978-0-7368-6441-1 (hardcover)
    ISBN-10: 0-7368-6441-5 (hardcover)
    1. Mummies—Juvenile literature. I. Title. II. Series
GN293.B47 2007
393'.3—dc22
                                                    2006001156

Editorial Credits
Aaron Sautter, editor; Juliette Peters, designer; Kelly Garvin, photo researcher/photo editor

Photo Credits
Capstone Press/Karon Dubke, cover, 4–5, 6, 7, 8–9
Corbis/Bettman, 24, 25; Charles & Josette Lenars, 12; CinemaPhoto, 27;
    Sandro Vannini, 13
Fortean Picture Library, 14; Dennis Stacy, 20; Kristan Lawson, 11
Getty Images Inc./The Image Bank/Gerard Rollando, 17; Taxi/Chip Simons, 28–29;
    Time & Life Pictures/Photo by Mansell, 18–19
Ingram Publishing, 16
ZUMA Press/The Movie Company, 22, 23; Universal Studios Hollywood, 26;
    Zuma Movie Stills Library, 21

Capstone Press thanks Tom Brooks and the staff of Meadowbrook Stables
in Mankato, Minnesota, for their help in making this book.

The author dedicates this book to her son Colin, who is just beginning to
find his own story.

Table of Contents

MONSTERS

Waking the Dead

Deep inside a dark pyramid, two scientists find a doorway. They peer into the gloomy tomb. Should they go in?

The scientists enter, eager to find the tomb's hidden secrets. They find a mummy inside. They carefully study the mummy's treasures. The mummy wakes and reaches out to grab them.

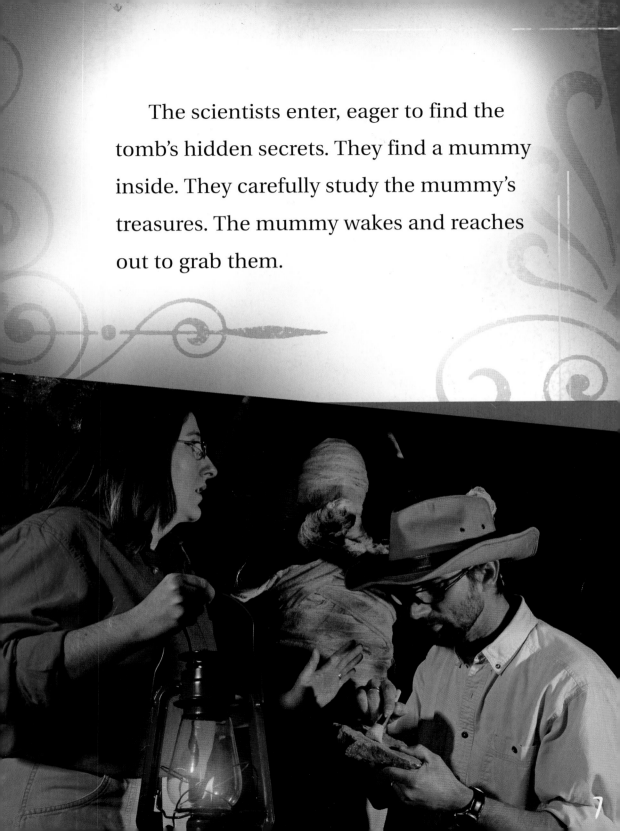

The scientists have disturbed the mummy's rest. The mummy grabs its victim! There is no escape from its deadly grasp.

The Mummy's Curse

Real mummies are found all over the world. Mummies are dead bodies that have been preserved. They can last for thousands of years.

BLAZER FACT

Scientists once found a 4,000-year-old mummy. Its bones were in near perfect condition.

11

12

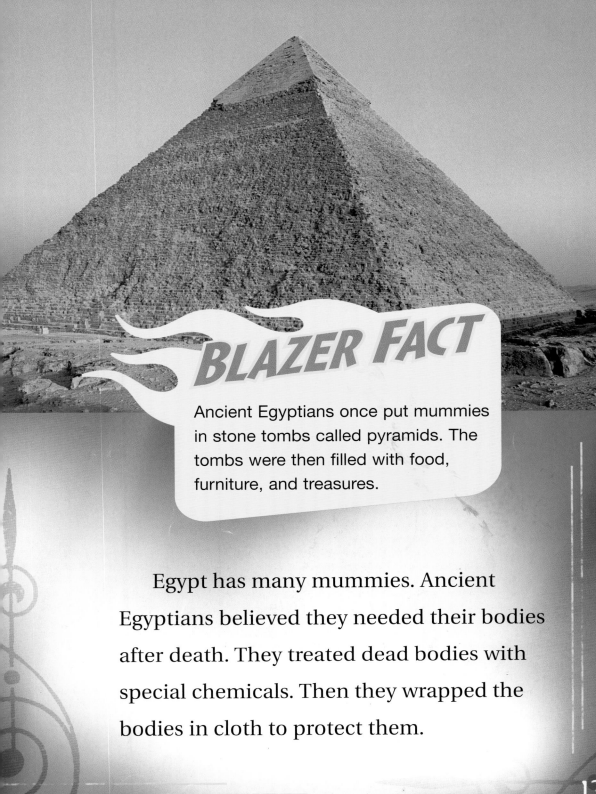

BLAZER FACT

Ancient Egyptians once put mummies in stone tombs called pyramids. The tombs were then filled with food, furniture, and treasures.

Egypt has many mummies. Ancient Egyptians believed they needed their bodies after death. They treated dead bodies with special chemicals. Then they wrapped the bodies in cloth to protect them.

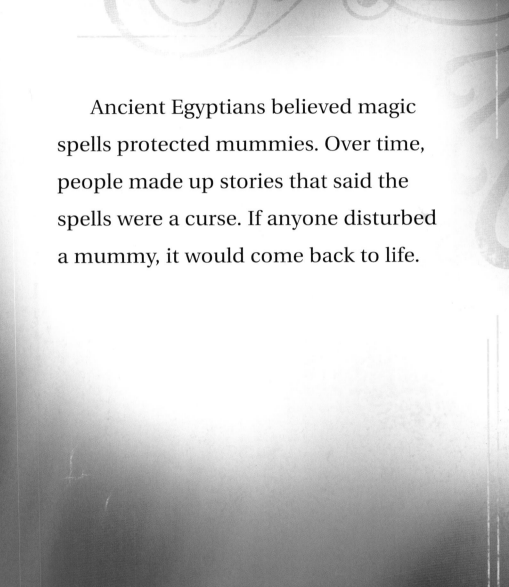

Ancient Egyptians believed magic spells protected mummies. Over time, people made up stories that said the spells were a curse. If anyone disturbed a mummy, it would come back to life.

Some stories said mummies were buried with a cursed scroll. The scroll also contained magic spells. If someone read from the scroll, the mummy would rise up to take revenge on that person.

BLAZER FACT

In 1923, scientists found King Tut's mummy. Soon after, some of the scientists died. Some people believed the mummy's curse had caused their deaths.

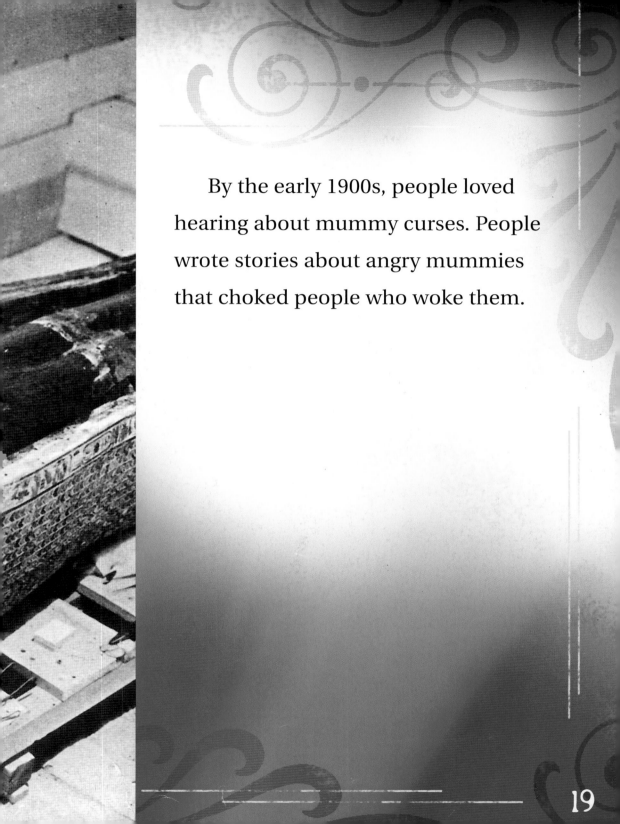

By the early 1900s, people loved hearing about mummy curses. People wrote stories about angry mummies that choked people who woke them.

Mummies aren't pretty. Many have been around for thousands of years. In stories, mummies walk stiffly. They stretch out their arms to grab their victims.

21

22

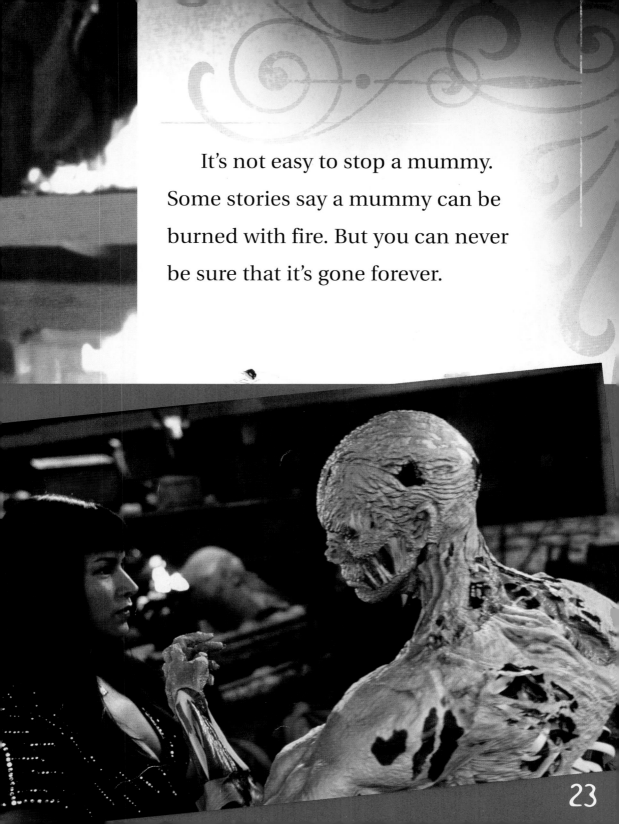

It's not easy to stop a mummy. Some stories say a mummy can be burned with fire. But you can never be sure that it's gone forever.

Finding Mummies Today

Mummy movies have been popular for many years. In most movies, few people ever escape the mummy's curse.

Mummies are usually scary in movies. But they can be fun too. Some mummy movies are funny. At theme parks, people dressed as mummies may reach out and try to grab you.

THEY'RE BACK! ...IN THEIR MUMMY'S ARMS!

BUD ABBOTT and LOU COSTELLO MEET The Mummy

with MARIE WINDSOR · MICHAEL ANSARA and PEGGY KING

Directed by CHARLES LAMONT · Screenplay by JOHN GRANT · Produced by HOWARD CHRISTIE
A UNIVERSAL-INTERNATIONAL PICTURE

27

Angry walking mummies are not real. Mummy curses are not real, either. But pretending that mummies are real can be fun!

Glossary

ancient (AYN-shunt)—belonging to a time long ago

curse (KURSS)—an evil spell meant to harm someone

preserve (pri-ZURV)—to protect something so that it stays in its original condition

revenge (rih-VENJ)—an action taken to repay harm done

scroll (SKROHL)—a roll of paper with writing on it

tomb (TOOM)—a grave, room, or building for holding a dead body

Read More

Burgan, Michael. *The Curse of King Tut's Tomb.* Graphic Library. Mankato, Minn.: Capstone Press, 2005.

Krensky, Stephen. *The Mummy.* Monster Chronicles. Minneapolis: Lerner, 2007.

Steer, Dugald. *Egyptology.* Ologies. Cambridge, Mass.: Candlewick Press, 2004.

Internet Sites

FactHound offers a safe, fun way to find Internet sites related to this book. All of the sites on FactHound have been researched by our staff.

Here's how:

1. Visit *www.facthound.com*

2. Choose your grade level.

3. Type in this book ID **0736864415** for age-appropriate sites. You may also browse subjects by clicking on letters, or by clicking on pictures and words.

4. Click on the **Fetch It** button.

FactHound will fetch the best sites for you!

Index